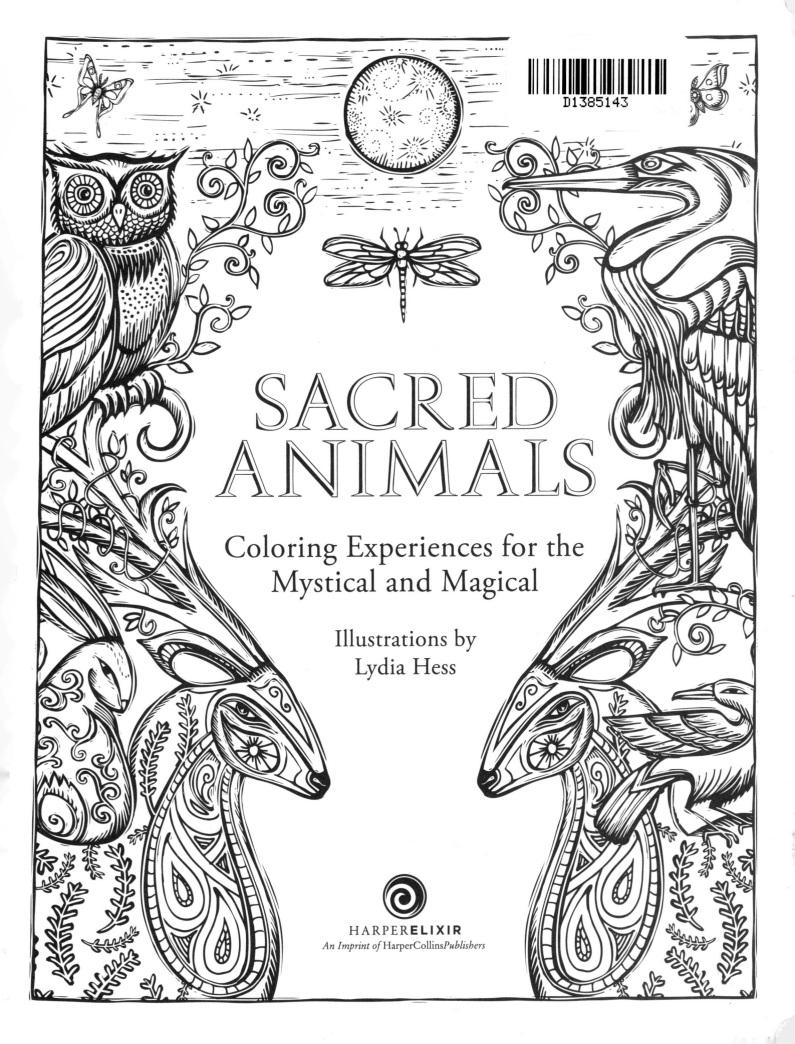

SACRED ANIMALS

Coloring Experiences for the Mystical and Magical

Illustrations by
Lydia Hess

HARPERELIXIR
An Imprint of HarperCollinsPublishers

This book is dedicated to my family.

My husband, Robbie, for his steadfast

support and encouragement;

and my two daughters, Tucker and Aubrey,

for their creative consultations.

HarperCollins books may be purchased for educational, business, or sales promotional use.
For information please e-mail the Special Markets Department at SPsales@harpercollins.com.

HarperCollins website: http://www.harpercollins.com

FIRST EDITION
Designed by Lydia Hess
Library of Congress Cataloging-in-Publication Data is available upon request.
ISBN 978–0–06–256383–5

16 17 18 19 20 BRR 10 9 8 7 6 5 4 3 2 1

Welcome to *Sacred Animals*. As you set out on a mystical journey of self-discovery that bridges worlds both within and without, we invite you to contemplate the timeless grace, strength, and quiet power embodied in these images. The wildness and profound beauty of animals—both real and imagined—have inspired humans for untold millennia. Long before we could write or record our histories, we painted, etched, and carved images of our animal brethren on our landscapes and shelters, incarnations of the mysteries and power of the natural world. Over time, animals—with their purity of emotion—have come to serve as symbols of the traits we hope to find within ourselves and of our connection to that which is greater than us. Our hope is that as you color, your mind quiets and your everyday cares recede as your soul expands.

LYDIA HESS

GROWTH

· ·

Stag

ENERGY

. . . .

Honeybee

TRANQUILITY

Fox

POWER

····································

Tiger & Butterfly

STRENGTH

Bison & Owl

RENEWAL

· ·

Snake

GRACE

· ·

Heron

PATIENCE

. . . .

Turtle

INSIGHT

· ...

Crow

MAGIC

· ·

Cat

INTUITION

· ·

Moth

LYDIA HESS

COURAGE

. . . .

Dragon

DETERMINATION

. . . .

Salmon

LYDIA HESS

INTELLIGENCE

· ····

Goat

TRUST

· ···

Porcupine

TRANSFORMATION

· ···

Frog

ABUNDANCE

Hare

FLUIDITY

· ·

Octopus

PURITY

· ···

Unicorn

INNOCENCE

Mouse

WONDER

. . . .

Humpback Whale

HONOR

· ·

Elephant

TRANSCENDENCE

Phoenix

REBIRTH

. . . .

Beetle

HONESTY

. . . .

Rooster

PRESENCE

· ...

Bear

INTEGRITY

· ···

Peacock

RESILIENCE

· ···

Gecko

POSSIBILITY

· ···

Pegasus

SPIRIT

· ·

Wolf & Cicada

VISION

· ·

Bat

LYDIA
HESS

TENACITY

· ···

Cow

FORTITUDE

· ···

Hippocampus

PRUDENCE

· ...

Squirrel

CLARITY

· ·

Orca

HOPE

· ···

Dragonfly

BRAVERY

· ·

Boar

LYDIA·HESS

KINDRED

· ...

Tree of Life

THE
END